IRELAND AND ITS ELSEWHERES

Ireland and Its Elsewheres
Harry Clifton

A collaboration between
THE IRELAND CHAIR OF POETRY
and
UNIVERSITY COLLEGE DUBLIN PRESS
Preas Choláiste Ollscoile Bhaile Átha Cliath
2015

First published 2015
UNIVERSITY COLLEGE DUBLIN PRESS
UCD Humanities Institute
Belfield
Dublin 4
www.ucdpress.ie

ISBN 978-1-906359-90-4
ISSN 2009-8065 The Poet's Chair series

CIP data available from the British Library

The right of Harry Clifton to be identified as the
author of this work has been asserted by him

Typeset in Adobe Kepler
Text design and setting by Lyn Davies Design
Printed in England on acid-free paper
by CPI Antony Rowe, Chippenham, Wiltshire

Contents

The Chair

for Mary Clayton

That commonest of objects, a chair –
I relax into it, gradually,
After a lifetime. The dream upholsters itself,
The peace, the thousand-yard stare.
The room is nothing, a box
Full of silence, with an empty shelf
For books, a tangle of flex,
A metal desk and a plastic telephone.
Everything else I bring in here
Is totally my own –
Exhaustion, memory, habit, desire.
As for the young, they have more to do
Than knock on my door. And what advice,
If any, could I give them?
O deep deep chintz, passivity
At last… I close my eyes,
I am on a flight, there is nowhere to go,
And yet, I am in mid-air
Suspended, possessionless,
Undeserving, somehow in first class –
They have given me the chair.

FOREWORD

We live in a time when the arts, and culture generally, are often portrayed as being somehow marginal in people's lives, as less than central. Worse, they are sometimes seen as being for an 'elite'. And public discourse can follow that line to its inevitable conclusion.

It is, of course, a wholly false characterisation – of the arts and of people. Everybody has a cultural life and everybody's life is engaged in one way or another with the arts, even if we do not always associate the things that we do with them. History and language have tended to distance the notion of the arts from the everyday life of all the people. But that everyday life is inextricably connected to the arts.

These truths, and truths they are, have considerable implications for public policy. The recognition of the essential part that arts and culture can play in the development of every person, of the richness that they can bring, of the fact that they can transform lives, can have profound consequences. The arts matter because people matter. And it is impossible to contemplate people as separate from an engagement with the arts.

The establishment, and the continuing existence of the Ireland Chair of Poetry, was and is a challenge to false assumptions. Initiated as a response to the award of the Nobel Prize to Seamus Heaney, it has become much more than that. It celebrates Heaney's achievement, of course, but it also offers the opportunity to acknowledge contemporary excellence in the work of those appointed to hold the Chair. It recognises the poetic tradition on the island of Ireland and the value and vitality of the poetic community. And, crucially, it proclaims the enduring importance of the prophetic voice of the poet and re-centres poetry in the public life of the people.

In discharge of that duty, it has since its inception, as a central part of its purpose, had a public role through the lectures, the engagement with students in the three Universities (QUB, TCD and UCD) and in the wider range of commitments that each of the holders of the Chair has embraced. Speaking before one of his public lectures in Trinity College, Dublin, the Professor whose lectures are collected in this volume spoke of the importance he attached to the link that the position offered between the 'Alexandrian world of scholarship and the rag and bone shop of the heart where poems are made'.

In those words Harry Clifton captured something central in the essence of the Ireland Chair of Poetry. It falls to the Trustees and their successors to give continuing life to that challenge and, in the process, to sing, and louder sing the place and potential of poetry and, by extension, of all the arts.

It is a pleasure to thank those who brought the Ireland Chair into being, to record appreciation of the commitment of the current Trustees and of the work that has brought this handsome volume to its public, as it is once again to express appreciation to the two Arts Councils and the three Universities for their continuing committed support of the project.

As ever, honour is due to the achievement and the memory of the man whose Nobel laurels prompted the establishment of the Ireland Chair of Poetry.

BOB COLLINS
Chair of the Board of Trustees, Ireland Chair of Poetry
September 2015

Seriously into Cultural Detritus
Writing the Rustbelt in Britain and Ireland

Here are some lines from a poem by Michael Donaghy, the one American among a group of poets, Scottish, English, Irish by derivation, who came together twenty years ago, in the London of the late eighties, early nineties. It is called 'Shibboleth' and describes a world where people are shot for not understanding certain passwords into modern, or postmodern life.

> One didn't know the name of Tarzan's monkey.
> Another couldn't strip the cellophane
> From a GI's pack of cigarettes.
> By such minutiae were the infiltrators detected.

I too lived in London, and was part of its cultural clutter of brand-names and icons, where no-one gets shot but many die of loneliness, for not understanding the modern shibboleths. Michael and I met in the Troubadour at Earls Court where I was reading with another of the group, Don Paterson, then about to publish his first collection *Nil Nil*. I was aware of Mike and Don through the journal *Poetry Review* for which I had begun writing criticism, but not aware of them as musicians until they came together for a bodhrán and guitar interlude between the readings. I understood then the importance of traditional music in their friendship, and later on its importance to the group in general.

It is worth remembering that Britain at this time was at an end and a beginning. The end of a decade of Conservative government under Margaret Thatcher, in which the unions had been crushed, the industrial communities in the north of England, in the shadow of their own gantries, pitheads, derricks and slagheaps, destroyed and embittered, against a larger background of expansionist capitalism under Ronald Reagan and the collapse of Soviet Communism. London, though depressed, had not yet seen the advent of New Labour which was to happen after the surprise defeat of Neil Kinnock by John Major in April 1992, the subject of an ambivalent poem by another in this group, Sean O'Brien.

When I walk by your house, I spit.
That's not true, I intend to.
When you're at breakfast with the *Daily Mail*
Remember me. I'm here about this time,
Disabled by restraint and staring.
But I do not send the bag of excrement,
Decapitate your dog at night
Or press you to a glass of Paraquat
Or hang you by your bollocks from a tree,
Still less conceal the small home-made device
Which blows your head off, do I, prat?
I think you'll have to grant me that.
Because I haven't. But I might.
If I were you, I'd be afraid of me.

['The Politics Of']

The stance, neither hard Left nor part, as yet, of the establishment, is very much of its time, when the independent and socialist bookshops still held on, and intellectual life had yet to be privatised. The poetic Right had lost its champion, Philip Larkin, in 1985. The laureate Ted Hughes was writing mainly in prose. There were no new names at Faber and Faber, though an Australian writing long, sprawling lines – Les Murray – and an all-inclusive yea-saying American poet dead since the sixties – Frank O'Hara – were making their influence felt. In damp, depressed London, culturally and politically, there was something of a power vacuum.

Meanwhile, at *Poetry Review*, Peter Forbes ran a broad church, liked by many who were to end up anthologised in *The New Poetry* published, not in London for a change, but in Newcastle by Bloodaxe Books – and despised, I think, by Oxbridge poets and critics perhaps feeling, for the first time, a slow but seismic shift beneath their sense of entitlement. The anthology survived supercilious reviews from the London elite and became a poetry bestseller, but is best seen now as the revenge of the post-industrial north on the effete south, and more importantly for my own purposes here, as a high tide of post-modernism, where ideas of Japan, Africa or Mexico mean more than the reality of those places and exist to be deployed in situations closer to home, as a form of social criticism. I could instance poems in this vein by any of the above names, but I am thinking in particular of another member of the group, the Leeds-based Ian Duhig, whose meditations on power I first came across in this anthology, such as 'Fundamentals', an Africa of the mind in which power and religion are inextricably mixed:

> Brethren, I know that many of you have come here today
> Because your Chief has promised any non-attender
> That he will stake him out, drive tent-pegs through his anus
> And sell his wives and children to the Portuguese.
> As far as possible, I want you to put that from your minds.
> Today, I want to talk to you about the Christian God.

Of others in the anthology, Simon Armitage had already been taken up by the London establishment, while the work of Peter Reading had hardened, rather too grimly and programmatically, into an anti-estab-lishment anti-poetics. But between these extremes, a group could be seen to be forming, of Celtic background cast adrift in different post-industrial landscapes from Donaghy's Bronx to Paterson's Dundee and the Leeds of Ian Duhig. Their senior and sometime mentor Sean O'Brien, though, is the one whose poem 'After Laforgue' provided the real introduction to their underlying ethos:

> I have put a blockade on high-mindedness.
> All night, through dawn and dead mid-morning,

Rain is playing rimshots on a bucket in the yard.
The weatherman tells me that winter comes on
As if he'd invented it. Fuck him.

From the defiant announcement of that first line and the chosen
demotic of the last, we have left behind the well-mannered discourse
of a certain university-educated poetry. In the third line, 'Rain is playing
rimshots on a bucket in the yard', we have also left behind the standard
five-beat line for one that breathes, talks, deals in black but accessible
vernacular wit, and incidentally, in the word 'rimshots' sends out the
signal of musical insiderishness, hipness even, that all these poets have
in common.

The drift is north, to the run-down seaports and icy termini of Hull,
Bradford and Newcastle, the mood one of black irony, the landscapes
strangely generalised, pre-apocalyptic, shot through with brand-names,
overhung with a death-wish of Arctic drizzle:

Teach me the weather will always be worsening,
With the arctic fleet behind it –
The subject of talk in the shop, at the corner,
Or thought of when stepping out into the yard
To the sirens of factories and pilot-boats,

There like a promise, the minute at nightfall
When rain turns to snow and is winter.

['After Laforgue']

And yet, paradoxically, we feel we have been here before. Isn't that
'rimshot' out of Philip Larkin, not to mention the obscenities, and the
'bricked-up boiling' in his poem 'Going, Going'? And doesn't the long,
conversational line have its origin in the Australian Les Murray? Aren't we
witnessing a man of the Left deriving his poetic line and to an extent his
vision from two men of the Right? Nor do the paradoxes end there, for the
'blockade on high-mindedness' in the first line is preceded by a title 'After

Laforgue' that advertises its author's familiarity with high culture and wants to situate his demotics in a distinguished, if ironised, line of European culture. This is a poet with a point to prove – that tough social origins and intellectual sophistication, if properly mixed in a poem, are a positive essence. And in this he lays down a template for the rest of the group.

One of these, and probably the most prominent to date, is Don Paterson, who narrowly missed inclusion in that Bloodaxe anthology in the crucial year 1993 when his own first book *Nil Nil* inaugurated a career that quickly dispensed with the need for inclusion in any anthology. Again, a northerner coming south from the rustbelt of Dundee, an ambivalent relation with the socially privileged London literary world, a vision of British apocalypse glimpsed, as with so many of these poets, from a train, like George Orwell's in *The Road to Wigan Pier*:

> you file past the stations
> sealed up between wars, like family vaults;
> though you make out the posters for Eye salts and Bloater Paste
> [...]
> you uncover the names of decanonized saints
> and football clubs, now long-extinct.
> [...]
> a slack river drags itself under the hills
> where the sheep swarm like maggots. These were the battlegrounds
> abandoned in laughter, the borders no more
> than feebly disputed; a land with no history,
> there being no victors to write it.
> [...]
> You pass the closed theme-park, a blighted nine-holer,
> the stadium built for a cancelled event
> [...]
> a smatter of gunfire pinks at your cheek
> as it leans on the glass. Now the line curves
> over pitheads and slagheaps, long towns with one street
> [...]

A station draws up, and slots into place
to fill the whole train with its name: C O W D E N B E A T H
[From Part I of 'The Alexandrian Library']

It is the landscape of Philip Larkin's 'Whitsun Weddings', northernised, with the beer-and-cricket removed – post-historical, on its last legs, yet rendered, evoked, with a kind of affection. We have it too in O'Brien and Duhig, in Donaghy's visions of run-down Bronx bars or Chicago neon from the overhead El. The poem as a kind of talking book, released by those long, free lines to digress, be clever, include anything and everything, and by implication, to go on forever. And the poet as stand-up comedian, industrial dreck in the background, entertaining us with his existential patter. Once you get someone talking in a poem, as Robert Frost once said, there is no end to the possibilities, and a case in point, his own long digressive 'New Hampshire', illustrates the good and the bad of being your own stand-up comedian as well as poet.

Frost, as Michael Donaghy once observed, was corrupted into the rhetoric of John Fitzgerald Kennedy, and the poems of Paterson and O'Brien, in their talking manner, read sometimes like a rhetoric possible to imagine for Nye Bevan, Arthur Scargill and the Glaswegian union leader Jimmy Reed – but only if Frost's 'golden age of poetry and power' had happened on the Left instead of the Right. Like Frost, there is a singer as well as a talker in Paterson. Or to employ the music metaphors so beloved of this group, a maker of three-minute singles and a man who riffs endlessly. Both come together in his well-known 'A Private Bottling' where the first part, a closed lyric of whisky-tasting and erotic distancing, gives way, in the second part, to a long riff on the same theme. But his collections of the nineties, with post-industrial Scotland in the background, are really a self-cleansing of cultural modernism, and like his mentor O'Brien, a working through of class anger against not only the middle classes but the middle-class act of poetry itself:

But if you still insist on resonance –
I'd swing for him, and every other cunt

happy to let my father know his station,
which probably includes yourself. To be blunt.

['An Elliptical Stylus']

The demotics of that, the sense of an angry man bursting through his own too-well mannered metrics to say something direct, are echoed in the stand-up comedy, compassion and sheer cultural intelligence of his fellow-poet Ian Duhig, whose instinct is to rewrite history as written by the victors, be they Yeats with his high rhetoric, the academic language of scholars and historians, or the technical shorthand of acronyms. A founding text for Duhig might be Bertolt Brecht's 'A Worker Reads, and Asks these Questions':

Who built Thebes with its seven gates?
In all the books it says kings.
Did kings drag up those rocks from the quarry?
[...]

The Young Alexander took India.
By himself?
Caesar hammered Gaul.
Had he not even a cook beside him? ...

Someone wins on every page.
Who cooked the winners' banquet?
One great man every ten years.
Who paid the expenses?

[trans. Edwin Morgan]

Duhig, who ran a shelter for the homeless in Leeds, has never forgotten the strains of 'I am a Jolly Beggarman' from the folk-club next door, from which the beggarmen themselves were barred, and it is his way of making a song, a word, a tone of voice indict itself unconsciously, in the ear of a knowing underclass, that has made his poems what they are. Yeats's '1916' and present-day Leeds, with its social and religious tensions, would seem unconnected, yet the high rhetoric of one is played off against the gut reality of the other, in 'Brilliant', with its epigraph by the Kaiser Chiefs – 'Everything in Leeds is Brilliant':

I met him one brilliant day
coming with brilliant faces
from clinic at number 12a
on our way to more brilliant places.
Then, riding a bus into town,
I sorted the world out with Sid –
agreeing when all's said and done,
we said a lot more than we did.
And then we lamented the sport,
remembering better times bitterly
and how they were only too short.
All changed, changed utterly.

This bomber's Dad ran a chip shop
which fried not with dripping but oil;
on match days he stood on the Kop
with Sid, now Sidique, from the school –
they wrote his work up in the *TES*.
You'd think you knew what Sid dreamed
he showed such social-consciousness,
so sensitive his nature seemed.
But drugs had this other young man
Till his parents sent him to learn
At a madrassa in Pakistan.
He too has been changed in his turn.

The hearkening back to Yeats, however ironically, and the involvement in traditional music – not to mention the Irish names of so many in this group – beg the question of roots and origins underlying this post-modern post-industrial wilderness, whether in Britain or America, and seem to suggest Ireland as a kind of taproot back to lost human and communal values. So we find Michael Donaghy with his bodhrán coming back a little nervously as an Irish-American, to commune with that first world of the spirit:

> Musicians in the kitchen, Sunday morning in Gweedore.
> An American with a tape recorder and a yellow notebook.
> 'What was the name of that last one?'
> The piper shrugs and points to the dark corner.
> 'Ask my father.'
> The American writes 'Ask My Father.'
>
> ['The Natural and Social Sciences']

Only in its seaports however – Belfast or Dundalk – does Ireland approach the rustbelt experience the poets of Hull, Dundee or Liverpool write out of, that conjunction of defunct machinery, biblical apocalypse, high-street brand-names and the music and songs of childhood in the background. There are elements of it in the gantried Belfast of Ciaran Carson, with the *Titanic* in the background, but there is no *RMS Titanic* in his work. Instead there is the quintessential *HMS Belfast*, the prison-ship going nowhere, with its dream-cargo of 'protholics and catestants', trapped in their binary world. It is outsiders like the French Romanian poet Benjamin Fondane who died in Auschwitz, or the German Hans Magnus Enzenberger who have written *RMS Titanic* as an image of Western collapse, and it is a Polish intellectual, Czeslaw Milosz, who pointed to the sinking of that ship in 1912 as the first hint that Western hubris had over-extended itself into nemesis.

That generalised apocalypse, rather than its local variant, is perhaps clearer in the work of Alan Gillis, which pushes past its Cadbury Twist and Elvis Presley clutter to something more universal in the desolation, perhaps for no better reason than that he is younger and the sectarian element has been so thoroughly addressed already, in the work of his mentors. And the echo of Philip Larkin, that unacknowledged mentor to so many of his rustbelt contemporaries across the water, as in the Hull poem 'Here', is quite consciously acknowledged, indeed deliberately imitated and updated, in Gillis's own Belfast poem 'There':

> There Way Out signs
> rust quietly. There dead leaves bare the tree's design,
> thornbushes sharpen, militant jackdaws shiver
> on thin wires, policing the lash-cackled river;
> and past a station post, its generator hum,
> the loughside sluices pebbles, an ulcered tongue
> slithered over rent teeth. There you must earn your living
> locked in food-chains, frigid skylines unforgiving.

If, by contrast, the Dublin docks lacked the Orange myth of Harland and Wolff, they had a Green myth instead, of cattle-boats and emigration, to localise them, and the ghost not of Philip but of James Larkin and the 1913 Lockout as their Thatcherite tragedy. But the grain-scattered, crane-haunted quays of the North Wall never had their bard, the anthologies passed them by, and high capitalism, as in Britain, sanitised them into glass and steel financial centres. Only here and there, as in the Dundalk of Conor O'Callaghan's poem 'East', is there an angry attempt to wrench Ireland away from its pastoral myth, and have it partake, like any other rustbelt seaport, in the crisis of the spirit:

> But give me a dreary eastern town that isn't vaguely romantic,
> where moon and stars are lost in the lights of the greyhound track
> and cheering comes to nothing and a flurry of misplaced bets
> blanketing the stands at dawn is about as spiritual as it gets.

Whatever about Ireland, to be a poet of the old Left in Britain became difficult after Blair and Brown, on a centrist pro-American platform, brought New Labour into power in 1997, and we find the poets negotiating uneasily with systems of patronage, be they universities, awards, or publishing houses, that doubled the security while halving the anger. Notable on their acknowledgement pages are the number of poems commissioned by this or that arts or cultural body, and the responses, from Don Paterson's violent 'The Reading' to Ian Duhig's use of medieval chivalric poetry as an image of American ambitions in the Middle East under George Bush, betray the awkwardness of their situation. Sean O'Brien, in his poem 'The Commission', puts it plainly:

> Above all, let your work be proof
> That art still has a role,
> Which, after all, you must admit,
> Is better than the dole.

And Michael Donaghy's 'The Commission' illustrates the arbitrariness of favour under the right or the wrong arts council:

> By Christmas Pope Clement was dead.
> And all of my efforts to stay in his favour
> were wasted, which just goes to show
> how completely the stars rule our lives.

The bringing together, under a new Picador poetry imprint edited by Don Paterson – and carefully, not to say jealously, watched by rival groups sensing nepotism – of Duhig, O'Brien and Donaghy among others, gave strength to the idea of a cohesive group to which was soon added the work of a young man from Liverpool with another Irish name, Paul Farley, whose first book *The Boy from the Chemist Is Here to See You* contained all the old rustbelt elements, the same wit and formal excellence as his mentors, with a dash of drugs and clubbing culture that pushed it beyond the insidious success of his seniors to the status, almost, of a fashion accessory in cool Britannia:

> If Melville and Hawthorne had taken the same drugs
> what would they have made of the counting-houses
> all suddenly full of lasers and bass drums
> that pummel the sternum and stop down the iris?

What would they have made of this light show's finale
unexposed, as they were, even to the flashbulb,
or amplified breakbeats through 20K sound rigs
and scantily clad boys and girls going apeshit?

['Cream']

Fashionability, disappearance of political anger, beg a question. If they are working now from the inside, what, if anything, have these poets still to give? As another Liverpudlian with an Irish name once said, 'The Beatles are bigger than Jesus', and, without meaning to, set the seal of relativity on icons from Jesus to Che to Marilyn Monroe that hang on the walls of a couple in a Michael Donaghy poem called 'Black Ice and Rain':

Their black walls smirked with Jesus on black velvet
– Jesus, Elvis, Mexican skeletons, big-eyed Virgins,
Rodin's hands clasped in chocolate prayer –
[...]
Lighting a meltdown of Paschal candles,
she watched me. He poured the drinks rasping
We're seriously into cultural detritus.

Rescuing the poem from that detritus, getting it out from under Eliot's heap of broken images, may yet be the heroism of these poets. No more hitching a ride on the backs of heartfelt classics by Yeats, Larkin, Laforgue, or shufflings of icons like post-modern cards, but 'a going back to the laws', as the poet Michael Hartnett puts it, and not merely the laws of verse, but the certainty that some things are truer and realer than others, that an underlying vision is intact, that poetry is there not to mock but to celebrate existence. I am thinking of Don Paterson's 'A poem is a little church, remember, / you, its congregation, I, its cantor', from 'Prologue', an ironic poem, and how it mutates, one book later, into the pure praise of 'The White Lie', where the language has cleansed itself, like the best of the English metaphysicals, and runs clear of its old pollutants:

Only by this – this shrewd obliquity
of speech, the broken word and the white lie,
do we check ourselves, as we might halt the sun
one degree from the meridian

Then wedge it by the thickness of the book
that everything might keep the blackedged look
of things, and that there might be time enough
to die in, dark to read by, distance to love.

And I'm thinking of 'A Minute's Silence' by Paul Farley where fifty
thousand Liverpool supporters let their minds drift, for a moment, over
the sacralised gloom of their own city, its lives and deaths and their own.
Of the folk purity of 'The Lammas Hireling' by Ian Duhig, and of 'Snow'
and 'The Mere' by Sean O'Brien, about the quiet unused unusable pool of
pure existence that lies in the middle of everything. And most especially
the many poems of Michael Donaghy himself, that get beyond the
cultural detritus to what he calls 'the machinery of grace' on which every-
thing from music to cycling to sheer existence balances and depends.

If it doesn't, of course, I've fallen. So much is chance,
So much agility, desire, and feverish care,
As bicyclists and harpsichordists prove,

Who only by moving can balance,
Only by balancing move.

['Machines']

It was Czeslaw Milosz, a poet one wouldn't immediately associate with
the crises and concerns of these poets, who spoke of the irony and miserabi-
lism of poetry in our age as a kind of cliché, a buying into a myth of decline,
and the difficulty of pure praise, of re-establishing a vertical hierarchy of
meaning and value again from a flattened-out spiritual landscape. That, if
anything, is where the best work of these poets may yet be to come.

Twenty years have gone by. Michael Donaghy is dead, and the Left bookshops of north London where we both lived have long since closed. The bitterness of the defeated Left, with its dead pit-villages and post-industrial dreck, is part of British folk memory now, in some degree due to the poets themselves, whose destiny it was to straddle the end of the Cold War, the lifting of the Iron Curtain, the coming down of the Berlin Wall, and the inauguration, in Britain and elsewhere, of a new era of high capitalism, iced over by bland centrist politics, shot through with the panic of religious war.

The rest are well established now, in academic or editorial positions. They have helped each other, of course, and been resented for it, and it may be that their essential contribution – which I take to be a repatriating of the major poetic strand from America, a shaking up of British gentility, a beating of the sophisticates at their own game, but this time in the name of a silent underclass – has been made. If I think of them two decades back, an image of Auden's comes to mind. The small group, united for a while by intensity, humour, mutual regard, out of which some essential human value is brought into play. As the Russian poet Akhmatova said of another small group, the Acmeists, all you need nowadays is an ashtray and a spittoon. Or to paraphrase that in the words of Don Paterson – a kettle, a room somewhere, and a packet of digestives.

A transcript of a lecture given in Queen's University, Belfast, on 8 February 2011.

The Uncreated Conscience
Europe in Irish Poetry

In the summer of 1942, when as Patrick Kavanagh tells us 'the Germans were fighting outside Rostov', the poet himself, with sandwiches and whiskey packed for him by his brother, was fellow-travelling with a group of pilgrims at Lough Derg, in the heart of the neutral and Catholic Irish Free State. The poem which contains the above reference to the fighting in Europe and which was completed on Kavanagh's return to Dublin contains a second, less passing reference to outside events:

> All Ireland's Patricks were present on Lough Derg,
> All Ireland that froze for want of Europe.
>
> ['Lough Derg']

It might seem strange, an invocation of Europe from the green heart of Ireland at an hour when that continent, that civilisation, was tearing itself apart, perhaps forever. Especially so, as just over the border from Donegal, Monaghan and Cavan, Europe had in fact come to Ireland with a vengeance, in the flames and casualties of the Belfast air raids. But in poetry, as we know, Europe is rarely its current self, and Greece or Rome, to quote the Russian poet Mandelstam, only another name for man's place in the universe – to be invoked, in 1942, by a French philosopher like Simone Weil, against bombed-out cities and roads streaming with refugees, or a poet like Kavanagh, trapped in Ireland by the war, against the narrowness of a state still unsure of itself among the nations, taking refuge in isolationism, coming of age a few years later, or 'coming to conscience' as Thomas Kinsella describes it in 'Downstream', his evocation of being young and southern Irish in wartime.

The soil of other lands

Drank lives that summer with a body thirst.
Nerveless by the European pit,
Ourselves through seven hundred years accurst,

We saw the barren world obscurely lit
By tall chimneys flickering in their pall,
The haunt of swinish man.

A poem not accidentally reminiscent, in its terza rima, of Dante Alighieri, the poet of the European quest, and of Joyce, the first but not the last to equate Europe with the working out of the Irish conscience.

As it was, Kavanagh returned from his summer pilgrimage, wrote the poem 'Lough Derg' and gave it into the keeping of his brother Peter, where it remained, a private document, until published in the 1980s, in an Ireland mired in the regressions of the Northern Irish Troubles, and looking to America not Europe for rescue and resolution. All that though, and its cultural context, were far ahead in 1942, with Yeats dead in France, Joyce in Switzerland, Donnelly in Spain, Beckett on the run from the Gestapo, hiking south to the Vaucluse, and Francis Stuart in Berlin. Ireland at the time may have been neutral space, without a national carrier to its name, but air traffic control was already in place, and the strange limbo of the departure lounge, crowded with the ghosts of the still living as well as the dead.

Who was the girl I took to bed
That frightful day on the Eastern Front,
Who laid her shaved head on my bloodied arm,
Who shuddered and groaned, muttered and murmured of
Franz and Volodya
And of someone whom I used to know,
Later denied, later still begged forgiveness of?
I know all her pet names,

I've kissed her all over.
Never once would she whisper my name
Among the others, no matter how I begged her to.

That is called 'Lissik' by Francis Stuart and canvasses a kind of moral inadequacy on the Irish poet's part, faced with a larger and more terrible reality, in this case a girl seared by the carnage on the Eastern Front, that will not let him be part of its or her suffering. It can be read alongside 'Ireland', another wartime Berlin lyric by Stuart, this time looking back, for sanctuary and refuge, to the country left behind:

Over you falls the sea light, festive yet pale,
As though from the trees hung candles alight in a gale
To fill with shadows your days, as the distant beat
Of waves fills the lonely width of many a Western street.
Bare and grey and yet hung with berries of mountain ash,
Drifting through ages, with tilted fields awash,
Steeped with your few lost lights in the long Atlantic dark,
Sea-birds' shelter, our shelter and ark.

Just as the first of those poems, in its jagged free-form battle notation, reads, to paraphrase William Empson, like a style being learned from a despair, so the second hearkens back, in its melodious nature mysticism, to the Celtic Twilight of Colum, Clarke, Higgins, and behind them, the shade of the early patriotic Yeats. Taken together, and alongside the few poems left by Charles Donnelly before his death in the Spanish Civil War, they constitute small, often overlooked but crucial documents in the moral history of an Ireland 'coming to conscience', as Thomas Kinsella wrote, not by staying at home but by self-immolation in a European catastrophe, a failed adventure of mankind in its search, as Dante expressed it in his canto of Ulysses, for the earthly paradise. Or as another thirties exile from Ireland, the poet Samuel Beckett, put it rather backhandedly in a broadcast on Radio Éireann about Irish volunteers at a hospital in Saint-Lô after the war:

I mean the possibility that some of those who were in Saint-Lô will come home realising that they got at least as good as they gave ... a vision and sense of a time-honoured conception of humanity in ruins, and perhaps even an inkling of the terms in which our condition is to be thought again. These will have been in France.

That is a statement of the universal over the national and the local, and of the European, for all its trial and error in the human sphere, as the universal – the search, as I referred to it in Dante, for the earthly paradise. Ireland is the pure, the national, the realm of innocence, Europe the corrupt, the universal, the realm of experience. And to get from innocence to experience, a physical displacement is still necessary, mother putting the clothes of her exiled son in order, for the move abroad, from the blood and soil of the local, the instinctive, to the loneliness of the thinking self. And not alone in Ireland, but all over Europe, the same uprooting, the same move from instinct to consciousness, the same shift, at the beginning of the last century, from the peripheries to the empty centre.

Let no-one who has not lived there idealise cities like Paris, Rome, Berlin as other than the *belle époque* sterility of bourgeois districts on the one hand and the immigrant slums around railway stations on the other. If there is spiritual hunger, it has come from somewhere else, to do its work, hermetically, in a new kind of desert, that does not care whether it lives or dies, but liberates it, for that very reason, into the detachment and anonymity that are the necessary ground of imagination. Paris, Rome, Berlin – and flowing into them, between wars and revolutions, the fugitive intellect of newly independent Nordic, Slavic, Hispanic, African countries, not to mention our own. Some, like Beckett, staying a lifetime in that desert, others, like Mandelstam or Tsvetaeva, a while before going back to whatever fate the homeland represents. Others again, like Milosz or Rilke, passing through, or like Benjamin Fondane, deported to Auschwitz, or like Paul Celan, unable to stand the loneliness, going under in the Seine. But all, for a priceless moment, availing of the strange aesthetic distance such cities represent, to get their real work done. All except those who are trapped, like Kavanagh that summer of 1942, in a halfway house between the pull of the local and the need to universalise it.

> The battles where ten thousand men die
> Are more significant than a peasant's emotional problem.
> But wars will be merely dry bones in histories
> And these common people real living creatures in it
> On the unwritten spaces between the lines.
>
> ['Lough Derg']

If I seem to be concentrating on Kavanagh it is because, in his mixture of innocence and extreme sophistication, he stands at that moment at a crossroads like our own, between Ireland and Europe. And to stay with him briefly as he makes reference to 'the freshness and recency of Christianity' he finds on Lough Derg, is to beg the question in another way. For we can see increasingly now, that the Christian civilisation we seem to have been living through in Ireland was in fact a Christian moment, surrounded by the old Celtic gods on the one hand, co-opted for nationalist ends – and on the other, the classical gods and heroes modern Irish poetry has co-opted with a vengeance, and which are in fact other names for the powers and instinctual drives behind our secular humanism. So, a moment in Irish poetry, a summer in 1942, with a before that is Celtic and an after that is classical. And the way into it, paradoxically, is via that most Christian of poets, Dante himself, at the moment in the *Commedia* that T. S. Eliot sees as the shading over of the classical world into the Christian – namely, the twenty-seventh canto of the *Purgatorio*, where Virgil passes the pilgrim poet into the guidance of Beatrice:

> Son, the temporal fire and the eternal, hast
> thou seen, and art come to a place where I,
> of myself, discern no further.
>
> [trans. T. S. Eliot]

It would not be an exaggeration to say that modern Irish poetry finds itself at just that point in the *Purgatorio*, between the classical and the Christian. And the interesting thing is that the poets, instead of moving in the direction we expect from Dante, are moving in both directions. Some, like Michael Hartnett, Eiléan Ní Chuilleanáin, Paul Durcan, away from the secular into the religious, in the direction of Beatrice. Others, like the later Clarke, the later Heaney, much of Mahon, Longley, Muldoon, into the realm of Virgil, the world at once distantly classical and instantly recognisable to Irish poets working in it as our own liberally concerned secular humanistic field of activity.

If we live at a time when the old gods, if not the old authors, no longer have an intercessory role or are susceptible of direct invocation, it is worth asking why they have become so present again in Irish poetry. I mentioned them already as other names for what we now call sub-conscious powers, instinctual drives, but a likelier explanation is that they are there to universalise what would otherwise be local or personal emotions or situations. Frequently quoted in this regard is the poem 'Epic' by Patrick Kavanagh, where a local land feud is set against the seemingly larger threat of Hitler before being universalised with reference to one of the founding texts of classical literature.

> That was the year of the Munich bother. Which
> Was most important? I inclined
> To lose my faith in Ballyrush and Gortin
> Till Homer's ghost came whispering to my mind.
> He said: I made the *Iliad* from such
> A local row. Gods make their own importance.

The move, as in Kavanagh's two other poems about Homer, is away from the local, the emotionally entrapped, towards the universal, the classically detached. And so too with the later Austin Clarke, once his nervous breakdown and his futile engagement with Irish Catholicism had been cleared away and he could bathe, like the later Yeats, in the light and laughter of the classics – a laughter of the gods as displeasing, it has to be said, to Éamon de Valera as to Plato himself or any others who take too seriously the founding of ideal states. A dangerous liberated laughter, best banished altogether with Joyce and Beckett, or clamped down on at home, as happened to the satires of Flann O'Brien on the Irish language. Detachment, universality – as Kavanagh puts it in his poem 'Intimate Parnassus'

> Serenely
> The citizens of Parnassus look on,
> As Homer tells us, and never laugh
> When any mortal has joined the party.
> What happens in the small towns –
> Hate, love, envy – is not
> The concern of the gods.

The small towns, however, were soon to have their revenge. Within a single poetic generation, as Northern Ireland went up in flames, it was they who were enlisting the gods, and not the other way around. The myth-kitty, and not only the classical one, was being ransacked for local resonance. The gods found themselves speaking a Belfast patois, their underworlds commandeered for mid-Ulster crises of liberal conscience. The pull of the local in Irish poetry had reasserted itself. Territoriality, the naming of streets, the mapping of townlands – Kavanagh's 'Epic' in reverse, the universality of Homer co-opted into the local row. And so, in Michael Longley's poem 'Ceasefire', when the figures out of Greek myth finally embrace in reconciliation, we have been primed as to their whereabouts well in advance, and not only by the title:

> 'I get down on my knees and do what must be done
> And kiss Achilles' hand, the killer of my son.'

And when the watchman in Seamus Heaney's 'Mycenae Lookout' poeticises his response to the end of the Trojan War, we know without difficulty that we are on ground much closer to home:

I moved beyond bad faith:
For his bullion bars, his bonus
was a rope-net and a bloodbath.
And the peace had come upon us.

If I were asked, though, to name one figure from the classical tradition who stands behind much in contemporary Irish poetry, it would not be from the roll-call of male or female immortals with walk-on parts in the drama of atrocity or redemption, nor indeed Virgil himself, welcoming and saying goodbye on the threshold of Dante's heaven, but the ambiguous shade of the Latin poet Horace, as rarely invoked directly, as he is omnipresent by implication. The myth, as we remember, is of poetic brilliance sanctioned by the power of Augustus (whose cruelties are elsewhere) and underpinned by the wealth of Maecenas, with a gift of the Sabine Farm in Tivoli, east of Rome, to write and be at ease in. Freedom, then, with a question mark hanging over it. The too-beautiful poem, bought at too little a price to oneself, and indirectly, too high a price to others. If, with the Polish poet Aleksander Wat, we believe the real value of a poem to be not only, or not so much, in its untested truth and beauty as in the human price paid for the making of it, there can be few in contemporary Irish poetry, north or south, who have not been forced to question the privilege underpinning the space of making – the liberal space – made available to us. Explicitly so in the north, where history asked the question and a wealth of ironic distancing, Horatian obliquities, suggested themselves as a kind of firewall. Less explicitly, but just as really, in the south, with its grants and amenities, its subsidised dreamspace, where the reading of Horace's 'Parcus deorum cultor' ode as 'Anything Can Happen' has to carry the rider 'but not to me', and where that dreamspace can be dismissed by the Marxist critic Lukács as 'power-protected inwardness', and every lyric gesture begs the Horatian question.

Modern Irish poets, it should be said, are much more aware of Horatian compromise, caught between power and money, Augustus and Maecenas, than Horace himself ever seems to have been. The poet as self-hating liberal, guilty bystander, looking across at the watch-towers of sectarian history from what Seamus Heaney calls 'the free state of image and allusion', is rehearsed, as here in Paul Muldoon, almost to the point of monotony.

'Look, son. Just look around you.
People are getting themselves killed
Left, right and centre
While you do what? Write rondeaux?
There's more to living in this country
Than stars and horses, pigs and trees,
Not that you'd guess it from your poems.
Do you never listen to the news?
You want to get down to something true,
Something a little nearer home.'

['Lunch with Pancho Villa']

In Ireland, as elsewhere in Europe, that deadlock and stranglehold of Horatianism has been broken, but only at an ultimate cost. When Mandelstam in Russia wrote a diatribe called 'Fourth Prose' and passed around a piece of doggerel about Stalin, it was an anti-Horatian gesture, as it was when Pasternak, against the better judgement of his liberal friends, wrote and published in the West a bad novel, *Doctor Zhivago*. And in Ireland when Patrick Kavanagh, suicidally, debunked the Ireland myth in his essays and the violent, even unfair, editorialisings of *Kavanagh's Weekly* in 1952, it was an anti-Horatian gesture, as was, in the mid-seventies, the apparently ruinous decision of Michael Hartnett to abandon the compromised medium of English, and work instead in the purer, because disempowered, tradition of Gaelic.

I am nothing new
I am not a lonely mouth
trying to chew
a niche for culture
in the clergy-cluttered south.

But I will not see
great men go down
who walked in rags
from town to town
finding English a necessary sin
the perfect language to sell pigs in.

['A Farewell to English']

All these anti-Horatian gestures involve the same elements: bad art, apparent coarseness as a necessary mode of breakout, the subsequent freedom to do their finest work, and the paying of an ultimate price. They satisfy Aleksander Wat's prescription for poetic authenticity, and give the lie to Horace.

The 'clergy-cluttered south', turned in on itself since independence, is where I and my generation came of age in the seventies and eighties, swept over by that wave of translated European poets I mentioned before, haunted by their comings and goings from the then cultural centres of Europe, their often terrible deaths on return to their homelands, but most of all their air of ethical authenticity, of having something to write and define themselves *against*. If they were Holocaust witnesses or Hermetics, they might find themselves echoed in the broken grammarless images, the deep subjectivity, of an Irish poet like Peter Sirr in his 'After a Day in the History of the City':

What vagabond bones
and you too, Ivar the Boneless,
come together now
stench of what plagues
thriving again
and everywhere one turns
places of execution

If they were angry refuseniks, the gentle satire of 'No Thanks' by Dennis O'Driscoll might seem a long way off, but they would have given it, if not its matter, at least its repeated manner.

No, I don't want to drop over for a meal
　on my way home from work
No, I'd much prefer you didn't feel obliged
　to honour me by crashing overnight
No, I haven't the slightest curiosity about seeing
　how your attic conversion finally turned out

Not exactly the *non serviam* of James Joyce. And the search for something to refuse, usually via Mandelstam or Milosz, who had found it impossible to publish in their own society, was given added irony by the fact that Ireland, as O'Driscoll has pointed out, was and is one of the easiest countries in which to publish a collection of poems. The sheer absence of pressure needed, artificially, a myth of resistance or dissidence to intensify it. Which is why perhaps, in the historically pressured space of Northern Ireland, that particular European graft did not take. A characterisation by one Northern Irish academic of Irish expatriate poets – jokingly of course – as veterans of the Amsterdam sex industry, reading Jean Baudrillard and working in Irish pubs in Prague, would only be possible in a context that had closed itself off, localised the old gods, and borrowed its self-image from Britain.

Another European decadent, Charles Baudelaire, once observed that there is no such thing as moral progress. As the remarks by the above academic indicate, there is no such thing as progress in Irish poetry either. The same features – decadence and pretentiousness – which caricatured earlier generations of the Irish thinking self in Europe, are still the caricature. Post-independence, the small insecure nation forages instead for identity in its own dark past, anthologising itself again and again, in the Bergsonian sense, as a closed not an open society, overcompensating, like pre-totalitarian Germany in the twenties, with folk dreams, beer-hall raucousness. Anyone endorsing such texts should remember that their Polish, Russian or Lithuanian equivalents, if they ever appeared, would exclude such thinking spirits as Milosz, Mandelstam, Herbert, Wat and Brodsky, and for the same anti-cosmopolitan, Europhobic reasons.

As John Butler Yeats once wrote to his son, a poet is not a lyricist. To which may be added, with examples from Colum, Higgins, Clarke and a host of others, there is nothing that decays quicker than Celtic Twilight lyricism, or any other lyricism, with the intellectual spine removed. That Irish poetry, to this day, identifies with its lyric self, is what sends its thinking self elsewhere, to do its work in the deserts of old European cities. But then, we were always a country exporting its complexities, whether sexual and economic, or poetic and spiritual, as a way of *not* thinking about them.

> All happened on Lough Derg as it is written
> In June nineteen forty-two
> When the Germans were fighting outside Rostov.
> The poet wrote it down as best he knew
>
> [Patrick Kavanagh, 'Lough Derg']

But which poet, and which pilgrimage? The one through Leitrim and Pettigo to Lough Derg, or the one we live in now, left out of Irish narratives and anthologies, that stumbles and sings itself, exiled out of instinct to a wider, lonelier consciousness, on the roads of Europe, through Burgos and Santander to Santiago – secular, disinherited, yet to find its Dante, its Chaucer, its Patrick Kavanagh? Are we talking here of a historical moment in the summer of 1942, or what Kavanagh elsewhere calls 'the eternal moment', with Ireland innocent, green, forever turned in on itself, on the edge of the universal?

> It is summer and the eerie beat
> Of madness in Europe trembles the
> Wings of the butterflies along the canal.
>
> O I had a future.
>
> ['I Had a Future']

But Europe is neither a future nor a past. Poetically speaking, Europe is an eternal present, or, to paraphrase that line of Mandelstam quoted earlier, it is another name for a universal quest, before and after the quest for and consolidation of nationhood which so defines, limits and obsesses Irish poetry to this day – what Kavanagh called 'the Ireland myth' – and where the poet, that summer of 1942, found his own internal exile. A quest as old as time itself, for the earthly paradise, fought over that summer by the monster ideologies, and lost on every side. And the poem of that quest, whether in secular France, Nazi Germany, Soviet Russia or Catholic, now capitalist, Ireland, the quintessential modern poem, is Canto XXVI of Dante's *Inferno* where Ulysses the Wanderer goes, with his band of adventurers, behind the sun, and perishes in sight of the earthly paradise. But not before invoking for his human fellows, the timelessness, placelessness and universality of the quest.

Considerate la vostra semenza:
fatti non foste a viver come bruti,
ma per seguir virtute e canoscenza.

Or if 'canoscenza' is another name for that uncreated conscience Joyce wished to forge for his country:

Men, consider your origins.
You were not born to live like brutes
But to follow virtue and experience.

A transcript of a lecture given in Trinity College Dublin, on 12 February 2012.

Instead of an Afterlife
Irish Poets in American Space

In North America, in the autumn of 1985, I watched one day as students who seemed all future and no past were sunning themselves on the campus lawns of Iowa University. I had come there as Irish representative on the University of Iowa International Writing Program. As its director Paul Engle joked, the Irish, recognisable by tweeds and woollens even in the hottest weather, were all past and no future. That autumn of 1985 however, with China opening to the West after the death of Mao, it was Chinese writers who seemed to be the future. The Cold War, though no-one knew it yet, was ending. Engle, himself married to a Chinese writer, had other priorities than Ireland.

A man I recognised as Khmer was foraging, unnoticed, in a rubbish bin. I remembered working, three years previously, in refugee camps on the borders of Thailand and Cambodia, or Kampuchea as it had been renamed under the 'stone-age communism' of the Khmer Rouge. This man, an escapee from that American-created disaster, had come in through the back entrance of transit camps and Californian resettlement programmes, to begin again in the Midwest, while I myself had entered through the front lobby of a fellowship funded by the State Department. There we were, invisible to each other and those around us. Two of the newly dead, in the same American afterlife.

'Isn't this a great country?' I heard one student say to another a little later, in the lift of the writer's building. 'Absolutely,' the other replied, without irony. I was reminded of lines from the Polish of Czeslaw Milosz, a poet I had begun reading in those far eastern camps in the early eighties, another ghost translated from older worlds to a new metaphysical state.

I learned at last to say: this is my home,
here, before the glowing coal of ocean sunsets,
on the shore which faces the shores of your Asia,
in a great republic, moderately corrupt.

['For Raja Rao']

Unlike either of these ghosts, the Khmer or the Polish, I did not have language difference to bring into focus all the other differences between my own little republic and this great one. I had instead a history of misunderstandings in the same language – blandishments and Gaelic playactings going back at least two centuries, to when Thomas Jefferson and Thomas Moore, American president and Irish bard, took the measure of each other, and Moore penned his liberal lines against the Republican of the day:

Away, away – I'd rather hold my neck
By doubtful tenure from a sultan's beck,
In climes where liberty has scarce been nam'd,
Than thus to live, where bastard freedom waves
Her fustian flag in mockery over slaves…

['Epistle to Viscount Forbes']

Would an Irish poet, with a career to make in the United States, address an American president like that today? Whatever about power relations – and Jefferson was later to smile indulgently at the above lines – the weight of aesthetic prestige still lay on the other side of the Atlantic, and Moore's renderings of the American wilderness, as his carriage jolted north through Syracuse to Niagara Falls, were nearer to Wordsworth's reassuring sublime and Rousseau's dream of the noble savage, than the Zen emptiness of Gary Snyder's Rockies, or the inhumanism of Robinson Jeffers's Pacific coastline a century later.

Nor did the arrival, in velvet cape and knee-breeches, of the next Irish sensation, Oscar Wilde, do anything to remove the condescension. By now, though, a line had been drawn between marketable flamboyance in an Irish poet and his need not to give offence to his American paymaster – a line overstepped once or twice by Wilde, when the mask of the aesthete slipped, and the mercenary peeped through. A sleeping giant was awakening, dimly aware, especially after Walt Whitman's poetic breakthrough, that it would one day have global power and its own aesthetic as well. When Wilde, at a press conference, said 'I am here to diffuse beauty', a journalist was quick to challenge him. 'What about that grain elevator over there? Is that beautiful?' Wilde, and the whole of the Old World romantic imagination, retreated as tactfully as possible, remarking only 'I am too near-sighted to judge it properly.'

Hardly had one monocle departed than another arrived, in 1903, on a high tide of Irish nationalism. William Yeats, there to emphasise the power and vitality of Irish subject matter, and like Wilde, to lecture rather than read his own work. Certainly not to feed imaginatively, whatever about financially or politically, off the American scene. By the time he left, though, the conditioning elements of Irish poetic presence on that scene for the next hundred years were in place. The sense of having to tread carefully between rival elements in an Irish proxy war. The careful handling of persona (in Yeats's case, being seen as Irish though resident in London) and of what got back to Ireland. And the awareness, through his sponsor John Quinn, of America as an archival realm, a Pharaoh's tomb where life-work from an older world could be mummified and preserved, for a healthy return. A realm of stopped time, where Fenian enthusiasm for his Emmet lecture in New York on that first tour would trap his reputation for the ones that came after, in a place and by people for whom everything real had frozen long ago, at their hour of intense exile – and oblige him, like Irish poets in America ever since, to turn back the clock from Irish actuality and accommodate their hospitality, their nostalgia, and their terrible need.

That need, for an Irish poet to remain what an exiled, wealthy constituency wanted him to be, embodied itself a few years later in Yeats's protégé Padraic Colum. He came to New York in 1914 with his wife Mary, on a passport of folk rurality, authentic and ageless Gaelic culture. His stay of months that became a life, or an afterlife, of publishing and lecturing, his poetic self – something static and marketable – drawing on an imagined Irish past, answering the homesickness of others by sacrificing its own capacity for change, as in 'Fuchsia Hedges in Connacht':

I think some saint of Eirinn wandering far
Found you and brought you here –
Demoiselles! –
For so I greet you in this alien air!

More intriguing, and the true eyes and ears of poetic Irishness in its American afterlife, is the memoir *Life and the Dream* by his wife Mary, dissecting the components of that afterlife she and her husband had entered into. The New York boarding house, identical in every detail of furniture and decoration to its Old World counterpart, yet eerily stripped of pastness, materiality – a stage-set in an anti-gravitational void. Or the drawing-room faux pas of her husband's refusal of a cheque for reading his poems to the other guests, unaware that things given freely in an older culture were paid for here, like any other labour. Or the brash externalities of the Jazz Age, embodied in their friend the poet Hart Crane, who was to commit suicide a few years later. The shock and glamour of the American afterlife, its apparent solidity and its metaphysical weightlessness, remained outside the scope of Colum's folk poetry, to be registered, instead, in his wife's prose.

While both were establishing themselves in Chicago and New York, the twenties had become the first real American decade in Europe, with Eliot and Pound making inroads, and Frost, Williams, Crane, Tate and Cummings passing through, though still seen as representatives of an aesthetically provincial society, whatever its post-war wealth and influence in other spheres. When Yeats needed money, as in 1914 and 1921, he toured America; when he needed spiritual replenishment, it was still Ravenna, Urbino, London, Paris, Rapallo where he took the waters. Joyce, Beckett, MacNeice and in the thirties Donnelly and Stuart, all that enquiring poetic intellect in flight from Ireland, still moved east instead of west, though the wells of Europe, increasingly now, were poisoned. As MacNeice puts it in his poem 'Refugees':

Their glances
Like wavering antennae feel
Around the sliding limber towers of Wall Street
And count the numbered docks and gingerly steal

Into the hinterland of their own future
Behind this excessive annunciation of towers,
Tracking their future selves through a continent of strangeness.

Though by no means one of his finest, 'Refugees' is pivotal in some respects, coming as it does at the end of the thirties, and, some would say, of Europe itself. America, the new centre of civilisation, is really *seen* for the first time by an Irish poet who has lived, taught and fallen in love there, and most importantly, allowed it to form part of his poetic imagination. This time, unlike in Wilde, the grain elevator has come into focus, along with the docks, the skyscrapers and the fire-escapes, but also, behind them all, the unnerving vertigo of American space.

But do not trust the sky, the blue that looks so candid
Is non-commital, frigid as a harlot's eye.

The refugees, a carefully selected elite, disembark from the Old World to service the New, but their movement is more than migration. It is transmigration, a passing through death into an afterlife uncannily similar to the last one, but ungrounded.

The resurrected,
The brisk or resigned Lazaruses, who want
Another chance, go trooping ashore
[...]
they still feel
The movement of the ship while through their imagination
The known and the unheard of constellations wheel.

A century on from Moore, and fifty years after Wilde, a sense had begun to exist of what it meant to be 'crossing over'. Part political, an awareness not only of the generosity but also of the darker side of that continent, in its global operations, and the consequent need for strategic silence. Part financial, the high emoluments, the honours ventriloquised back to the Old World, the archival possibilities, but also the need to temper irony, outrageousness, in the presence of a sensitive, if sometimes under-respected patron. But mainly metaphysical, the replacement of time in the historical sense with some kind of shimmering flux in an eternal American present.

For a moment though, it is worth going back to that Iowa autumn of 1985 we began with. September becoming October, the leaves a brilliant yellow, the cornfields bare to the horizon. The new chill at night, the skin of ice on the river. The visiting writers in high boots and sheepskin coats, bought from stipends unimaginable in their African, Asian, Latin American countries. The busrides to the company buildings of billionaire sponsors to the programme, listening at the heads of tables as each writer in turn explained his origins, and the motto on the wall read 'Work Hard and Smile'. The hypochondrias out of nowhere, the goings into analysis. The paranoias at reports to the State Department in Washington DC. The erotic freedom, and the creative impasse. The affair between the beautiful Trotskyite from Mexico and the writer from South Africa. The Pole, unable to speak any English, drinking alone in his little room, an unhappy guest at what his fellow-exile, Czeslaw Milosz, called the Feast of Insubstantiality:

> Out of trees, field stones, even lemons on the table,
> materiality escaped and their spectrum
> proved to be a void, a haze on a film.
> Dispossessed of its objects, space was swarming.
> Everywhere was nowhere and nowhere, everywhere.
>
> ['Oeconomia Divina']

That sense, already evident in the prose of Mary Colum, of the self as an egg exploding outwards in a pressureless American vacuum, had

A lonely room.
                An electric fire
glowing in one corner. He is lying on his side.
It is late. He is at the centre of a city,
awake.
        Above and below him
there are other rooms, with others in them.
He knows nobody as yet, and has
no wish to. Outside the window
the street noises ascend.

His cell hangs in the night.

He could give up.
But there is something he must do.

Less political, more a reflection of otherworldliness, is the same poet's 'Crab Orchard Sanctuary: Late October', an evocation of the Midwest, through which the psyche, unmoored in American space, seems to drift by a lakeshore suburb at once completely ordinary, but also with its 'air at room temperature / like the end of the world', as if apocalypse, unnoticed, had already happened, and we were standing, beyond good and evil, on a farther shore of existence.

The car park was empty. Long threads of spider silk
blew out softly from the tips of trees.
[...]
A naked Indian stepped out onto the grass
silent and savage, faded,
grew transparent, disappeared.

Such are the attempts of one Irish poet to orient himself, politically and metaphysically, in that otherworld called America. But they are rare, and in other Irish poets almost non-existent. It is as if the poetic self, in mid-Atlantic, turned back, and only the pragmatic self flew on, to this or that earning-place, for its take-home pay. No political protest against Vietnam, the Central Intelligence Agency, the despoliation of the universe. No biting of the hand that feeds, and confers prestige. And yet the deeper protest is there, the metaphysical protest, though rarely explicit as in Kinsella's two poems. But implicitly, in the shrinking back of the Irish imagination from that American afterlife, to engage with its own local, physical, grounded existence, be it Kinsella's Inchicore, Montague's Tyrone, or the south Derry townlands of Seamus Heaney.

> We have no prairies
> To slice a big sun at evening
> […]
> Our pioneers keep striking
> Inwards and downwards,
>
> ['Bogland']

Or, if resident over there like Eamon Grennan, the need to earth imagination over here, as in his 'Mushroom-Picking in the Old World':

> You feel their foreign heartbeat in the grass:
> they are a firm spongy fullness in the hand, a rich
> smell overwhelming the house, a blessing of boiled milk
> and garlic. The phrase *fruits of the earth* fires
> in your head.

Anyone driving through Ireland since the nineties, with its four-lane highways, its filling stations and haulage roar, could be forgiven for thinking that big American externality had swept away inwardness and downwardness, the Irish pioneer delving quietly into what Kavanagh called his 'humus of repose'. Yet the New World had always been there, in the American comics arriving for the young returnee Montague on his Tyrone farm, or the wartime jazz and GI presence in Heaney's south Derry. But these things, in their poems, are registered only in retrospect, annexed, as it were like side-chapels, into the dominant Christian or Irish myths by which they and their generation still wrote and lived.

For a sense that America is there from the beginning, we have to move ahead a generation, to the young Paul Muldoon, who effortlessly incorporates into his work a pick and mix of mythologies, flicked though like television channels, each as real or unreal as any of the others. The American Civil War and the island of Alcatraz, in his early work, take their place alongside Kate Whiskey and Our Lady of Arboe as equal claimants on deep reality. And soon, with the reclusive billionaire Howard Hughes, the surfboard culture of California and the shape-changing Trickster-dom of 'The More a Man Has, the More a Man Wants', start to monopolise the foreground altogether. It is a long way from the evocations of the physical, the local, in Kinsella, Montague or Heaney, and yet it is being written by a young man in the backwardness and inwardness of Troubles Belfast, who has yet to turn his face to the New World and cross over.

> The Atlantic Club was an old grain-silo
> That gave onto the wharf.
> Not the kind of place you took your wife
> Unless she had it in mind to strip
> Or you had a mind to put her up for sale.
>
> ['Immram']

That grain elevator Oscar Wilde, replying to the journalist, was 'too near-sighted' to see, and which re-appears fifty years later as itself, in MacNeice's 'Refugees', is now, a further fifty years on, as cinematically clear as it is unreal, in a Bogartian scenario as believable for its creator as Jesus Christ was for his predecessors. Strictly speaking there is no need for the poet to go to America at all, for he already exists in a post-real, if not posthumous state of the soul he has moved over into, where everything, though perfectly in focus, is oddly affectless, stripped of value. A state of the soul already written of by the Polish émigré Isaac Singer, when he wakes to a hell of the spirit he has passed into, embodied by the dingy New York room he now inhabits, and cries out 'I am lost, lost in America!'

Not that everyone in America wakes to feel himself in hell, for some unknown transgression in the Old World, but the evidence of heaven is not that omnipresent either, and the sense, in so many Irish poets resident in or visiting America, of nostalgia for the physical, the local, the permanent, for the vertical hierarchy of values and the continuity of the self from one day to the next, cannot be entirely accidental. Wilde's grain elevator, a hundred years later, is now Derek Mahon's home from home in the 'alien nation' – but the place or state of mind, call it the Lower Manhattan waterfront or the wharves of Lethe, is still the same.

> a sense I get right here that Gansevoort
> has 'no existence, natural or real, apart
> from its being perceived by the understanding'.
> [...]
>   the skills of Venturi, Thomson, Rowse
> that can make post-modern a 19th-century warehouse
> and those of Hollywood *film noir* have combined
> to create virtual realities in the mind
>
> ['Global Village']

Whatever about heaven or hell, the American afterlife, for many Irish poets, has come to mean one thing in particular – artistic posterity. When an Irish president and her aides examined texts in a glass case at Emory University, it crystallised, in both tragic and comic senses, the Irish poet's wish to be posthumous, in his or her own lifetime. Tragic, in the sense of an Irish birthright, perhaps the last remaining birthright of a small nation in a globalised age, sold into a lucrative afterworld. Comic, as in a body put on ice, awaiting, perhaps a century later, a kiss of recognition, to awaken it into immortality. The organised archive, like Lawrence's ship of death, crossing over from Irish meanness of mind to final vindication on a farther shore, an America of the self-embalmed, a death before its time.

In the wintry dusk of December 1985, with the stadia lit up below me, the lights of cars along the Potomac, I flew in from Iowa to Washington DC, a guest of America, presenting himself to the State Department at the end of his stay. Untroubled by any report that might have been filed, for unlike the Chinese novelists, the lonely Pole in his room, the playwright driving the van for the writing programme to stay in America, I had somewhere to go back to. A man at the apex of fortune, as the nameless Khmer I had seen in September, adrift among rubbish bins, was touching its nadir.

And yet, with one thing in common. The memory of a refugee camp, three years back, in southern Thailand. Old Khmer women keening, their heads shaven, the betel juice staining their white robes, saying goodbye to their sons, as the buses for Panatnikom transit point, the Philippines and the New World waited, at the end of the ruinous American adventure in south-east Asia. A scene out of George Moore, not Tom Moore – an American wake, and an awareness, as they gave a blessing to their next re-incarnation, of a departure not to a future life, but to an afterlife.

A transcript of a lecture given in University College Dublin, on 20 February 2013.

HARRY CLIFTON was born in Dublin in 1952 and educated at University College Dublin. After graduating with an MA in philosophy, he left Ireland and worked in Nigeria and Thailand, returning in 1982; from 1988 to 2004 he lived in Italy, Switzerland, England, Germany and France. He published the pamphlet Null Beauty in 1976 and the books *The Walls of Carthage* (1977), *Office of the Salt Merchant* (1979), *The Liberal Cage* (1988), *The Desert Route: Selected Poems 1973–1988* (1992), *Night Train through the Brenner* (1994), *Secular Eden: Paris Notebooks 1994–2004* (2007) and *The Winter Sleep of Captain Lemass* (2012). His work has been translated into several European languages as well as Chinese. Harry Clifton won the Patrick Kavanagh Award in 1981, the *Irish Times* Poetry Now Award in 2008; he is also a member of Aosdána. He was Ireland Professor of Poetry from 2010 to 2013.

ACKNOWLEDGEMENTS

The author and publisher gratefully acknowledge the following for permission to reprint copyright material.

Michael Donaghy: 'Shibboleth' and 'Machines', from *Collected Poems* (Picador, 2009). Reprinted by kind permission of Picador.

Ian Duhig: 'Brilliant', from *The Speed of Dark* (Picador, 2007). Reprinted by kind permission of Picador.

Paul Farley: 'Cream', from *The Boy from the Chemist Is Here to See You* (Picador, 1998). Reprinted by kind permission of Picador.

Eamon Grennan: 'Mushroom-Picking in the Old World', from *Wildly for Days* (The Gallery Press, 1983). Reprinted by kind permission of the author and The Gallery Press.

Patrick Kavanagh: 'Epic' and 'Intimate Parnassus', from *Collected Poems of Patrick Kavanagh* (Penguin/Allen Lane, 2004). Reprinted by kind permission of Penguin/Allen Lane.

Sean O'Brien: 'The Politics of ', from *Collected Poems* (Picador, 2012). Reprinted by kind permission of Picador.

Peter Sirr: 'After a Day in the History of the City', from *Selected Poems* (The Gallery Press, 2004). Reprinted by kind permission of the author and The Gallery Press.

Francis Stuart: 'Lissik' and 'Ireland', from *We Have Kept the Faith: New and Selected Poems* (Raven Arts Press, 1992). Reprinted by kind permission of Raven Arts Press.

BIBLIOGRAPHY

Dante Alighieri, *Inferno* XXVI, 118–20 (Milan, 1987).

Samuel Beckett: 'The Capital of the Ruins', *The Complete Short Prose of Samuel Beckett 1929–1989* (New York, 1997).

Bertolt Brecht: 'A Worker Reads, and Asks these Questions', trans. by Edwin Morgan, from *Modern European Poetry* (New York, 1966).

Ciaran Carson, *Collected Poems* (Meath, 2008).

Mary Colum, *Life and the Dream* (Dublin, 1996).

Padraic Colum: 'Fuchsia Hedges in Connacht', from *Selected Poems of Padraic Colum* (New York, 1989).

Michael Donaghy: 'Shibboleth', 'The Natural and Social Sciences', 'The Commission', 'Black Ice and Rain', and 'Machines', from *Collected Poems* (London, 2009).

Ian Duhig: 'Fundamentals' and 'Brilliant', from *The Speed of Dark* (London, 2007).

Paul Farley: 'Cream', from *The Boy from the Chemist Is Here to See You* (London, 1998).

Alan Gillis: 'There', from *Hawks and Doves* (Meath, 2007).

Eamon Grennan: 'Mushroom-Picking in the Old World', from *Wildly for Days* (Meath, 1983).

Michael Hartnett: 'A Farewell to English', from *Collected Poems* (Meath, 2001).

Seamus Heaney: 'Bogland', from *Door into the Dark* (London, 1969).

_____. 'Mycenae Lookout', from *Opened Ground: Poems 1966–1996* (London, 1998).

Horace Odes, 'Book 1, xxiv', *The Complete Odes and Epodes* (Oxford, 1997).

Patrick Kavanagh: 'Lough Derg', 'Epic', 'Intimate Parnassus', 'I had a Future', and 'To Hell with Commonsense', from *Collected Poems of Patrick Kavanagh* (London, 2004).

Thomas Kinsella: 'Downstream', 'The Good Fight', and 'Crab Orchard Sanctuary: Late October', from *Collected Poems* (Oxford, 1996).

Michael Longley: 'Ceasefire', from *Collected Poems* (London, 2007).

Louis MacNeice: 'Refugees', from *Collected Poems* (London, 2007).

Derek Mahon: 'Global Village', from *New Collected Poems* (Meath, 2011).

Czeslaw Milosz: 'For Raja Rao' and 'Oeconomia Divina', from *The Collected Poems 1931–1987* (London, 1988).

Thomas Moore: 'Epistle to Viscount Forbes', from *Epistles, Odes and Other Poems* (Philadelphia, 1806).

Paul Muldoon: 'Immram' and 'Lunch with Pancho Villa', from *Poems 1968–1998* (London, 2001).

The New Poetry (Northumberland, 1993).

Sean O'Brien: 'The Politics Of ', 'After Laforgue', and 'The Commission', from *Collected Poems* (London, 2012).

Conor O'Callaghan: 'East', from *Seatown* (Meath, 1999).

Dennis O'Driscoll: 'No Thanks', from *New and Selected Poems* (London, 2004).

Don Paterson: 'The Alexandrian Library', 'An Elliptical Stylus' and 'The White Lie', from *Nil Nil* (London, 1993).

Peter Sirr: 'After a Day in the History of the City', from *Selected Poems* (Meath, 2004).

Francis Stuart: 'Lissik' and 'Ireland', from *We Have Kept the Faith: New and Selected Poems* (Dublin, 1992).

Translations, unless otherwise credited, are by Harry Clifton.